THE BOOK OF
BUNNY SUICIDES

VALEAS MUNDUM

ANDY RILEY HAS WRITTEN FOR BLACK BOOKS, TRIGGER HAPPY TV, SO GRAHAM NORTON AND SMACK THE PONY. HE HAS CO-WRITTEN THE BAFTA AWARD-WINNING ROBBIE THE REINDEER, THE RADIO FOUR PANEL GAME THE 99p CHALLENGE AND A DISNEY ANIMATION FEATURE, GNOMEO AND JULIET, TO BE RELEASED IN 2005. HE ALSO HAS A WEEKLY COMIC STRIP IN THE OBSERVER MAGAZINE.

THE BOOK OF
BUNNY SUICIDES

ANDY RILEY

A PLUME BOOK

PLUME
PUBLISHED BY THE PENGUIN GROUP

PENGUIN GROUP (USA) INC., 375 HUDSON STREET, NEW YORK, NEW YORK 10014, USA
PENGUIN BOOKS LTD, 80 STRAND, LONDON WC2R ORL, ENGLAND
PENGUIN BOOKS AUSTRALIA LTD, 250 CAMBERWELL ROAD, CAMBERWELL, VICTORIA 3124, AUSTRALIA
PENGUIN BOOKS CANADA LTD, 10 ALCORN AVENUE, TORONTO, ONTARIO, CANADA MV4 3B2
PENGUIN BOOKS INDIA (P) LTD, 11 COMMUNITY CENTRE, PANCHSHEEL PARK, NEW DELHI - 110 017, INDIA
PENGUIN BOOKS (NZ) LTD, CNR ROSEDALE AND AIRBORNE ROADS, ALBANY, AUCKLAND 1310, NEW ZEALAND
PENGUIN BOOKS (SOUTH AFRICA) (PTY) LTD, 24 STURDEE AVENUE, ROSEBANK, JOHANNESBURG 2196, SOUTH AFRICA

PENGUIN BOOKS LTD, REGISTERED OFFICES: 80 STRAND, LONDON WC2R ORL, ENGLAND

PUBLISHED BY PLUME, A MEMBER OF THE PENGUIN GROUP (USA) INC. THIS IS AN AUTHORIZED REPRINT OF A HARDCOVER EDITION PUBLISHED BY HODDER & STOUGHTON, 338 EUSTON ROAD, LONDON NW1 3BH, ENGLAND
FIRST PLUME PRINTING, JANUARY 2004

30 29 28 27 26 25 24

BOOKS ARE AVAILABLE AT QUANTITY DISCOUNTS WHEN USED TO PROMOTE PRODUCTS OR SERVICES. FOR INFORMATION PLEASE WRITE TO PREMIUM MARKETING DIVISION, PENGUIN GROUP (USA) INC., 375 HUDSON STREET, NEW YORK, NEW YORK 10014.

WITH THANKS TO

KEVIN CECIL, ARTHUR MATHEWS

AND ALSO...

POLLY FABER, CAMILLA HORNBY,
KATY FOLLAIN + AMANDA SCHOENWALD

FOR POLLY

* TWO RABBITS JUGGLING CHISELS DURING A TOTAL ECLIPSE OF THE SUN

EPILOGUE

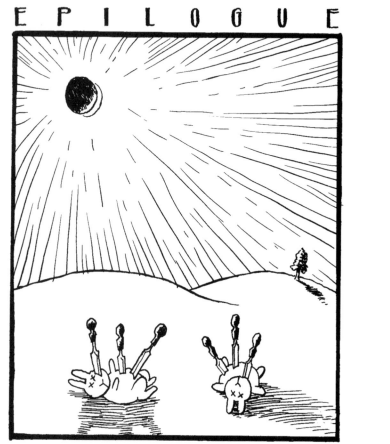

More Humor from the
"Wonderfully Deviant"* Andy Riley

978-0-452-28623-8

978-0-452-28624-5

Coming Soon!

978-0-452-29003-7

978-0-452-28703-7

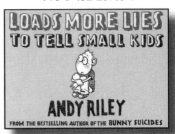

978-0-452-28856-0

* The Washington Post

 Plume * A member of Penguin Group (USA) Inc. * www.penguin.com